HINDU FESTIVALS COOKBOOK

D0791357

KERENA MARCHANT
WITH PHOTOGRAPHY BY ZUL MUKHIDA

HODDER
Wayland

An imprint of Hodder Children's Books

FESTIVALS COOKBOOKS

CHRISTIAN FESTIVALS COOKBOOK

HINDU FESTIVALS COOKBOOK

JEWISH FESTIVALS COOKBOOK

CHINESE FESTIVALS COOKBOOK

NB: Nuts are contained in some of the recipes in this book
(see pages 18–19, 20, 24–25, 26–27, 28).
Nuts may provoke a dangerous allergic reaction in some people.

© 2000 White-Thomson Publishing Ltd

Produced for Hodder Wayland by Margot Richardson
23 Hanover Terrace, Brighton, E Sussex, BN2 2SN, UK

Food photography: Zul Mukhida, Chapel Studios, Brighton
Design and illustrations: Tim Mayer
Proofreader: Philippa Smith
The recipe for Coconut Barfi (page 20) is adapted from *The Best of Lord Krishna's Cuisine* by Yamunda Devi (Bala Books Inc, California)

Published in Great Britain in 2000 by Hodder Wayland, an imprint of Hodder Children's Books. This edition published in 2001.

The right of Kerena Marchant to be identified as the author of this Work has been asserted by her in accordance with the Copyright, Designs and Patents Act 1988.

Picture acknowledgements:
Art Directors and TRIP 6 (H Rogers), 22, 23 (H Rogers); Eye Ubiquitous 5 (David Cumming); Impact Photos 4 (Mohamed Ansar), 13 (Christopher Cormack), 14 (Mohamed Ansar), 21 (Mohamed Ansar), 29 (Christopher Cormack); Christine Osborne Pictures 15; Gettyone/Stone 7 (Paul Harris).

All instructions, information and advice given in this book are believed to be reliable and accurate. All guidelines and warnings should be read carefully and the author, packager, editor and publisher cannot accept responsibility for injuries or damage arising out of failure to comply with the same.

All rights reserved. No part of this publication may be reproduced, stored in a retrieval system, or transmitted, in any form or by any means without the prior written permission of the publisher, nor be otherwise circulated in any form of binding or cover other than that in which it is published and without a similar condition being imposed on the subsequent purchaser.

A catalogue record for this book is available from the British Library.

ISBN 0 7502 3322 2

Printed and bound in Italy by G. Canale & C.S.p.A., Turin

Hodder Children's Books
A division of Hodder Headline
338 Euston Road, London NW1 3BH

CONTENTS

HinDU Festivals anD FooD

The Hindu religion started in India. Hindus believe in one god, but worship him in many different forms. The main ones are Vishnu, Shiva, the Goddess Shakti, Prince Rama and Krishna. Because there are so many gods, there are many Hindu festivals during a year. They celebrate the birthdays or deeds of the gods.

Food plays a big part in Hindu worship. During festivals, the worshippers offer the gods' or goddesses' favourite foods to them and then share it among themselves. Most of the gods are believed to have a sweet tooth so sweets and puddings often feature on the menu at festivals.

The gods do not only get fed at festivals. Before sitting down to a meal, Hindus will offer some of the food they are about to eat to the gods. This food is called *prashad*. In the home, it is placed before the pictures or statues of the gods.

When Hindus visit a temple, they always bring *prashad* with them, especially at festival time.

Hindus are mostly vegetarian and do not eat meat. This is because Hindus believe in reincarnation: that when they die they are reborn as another human being or even an animal, bird, fish or insect. To eat an animal or a bird might mean eating the soul of a human being about to be reborn.

Hindus eat meals with their right hand instead of using cutlery. At this wedding feast in India, the food has been served on banana leaves.

The cow is regarded as a holy animal because the god, Krishna, loved cows. A Hindu will never kill a cow or wear leather that comes from a cow. Milk and dairy products are believed to have strong spiritual powers and are always offered to the gods at festivals.

Traditional Hindus will only eat food that has been cooked by them, their immediate family or close friends. On a journey, they will only eat food that they have prepared. When Hindus emigrated from India they continued to eat their traditional food. They did not eat the food of the countries where they went to live. This is why Hindu food remains the same all over the world.

SAFETY AND HYGIENE

When cutting with knives, frying, boiling and using the oven, ALWAYS ask an adult to help you.

Food must always be kept clean. Food that gets dirty will not taste good – and can even make people sick.

Always wash your hands before you start cooking.

Do not wipe dirty hands on a towel. Wash your hands first.

If you need to taste something while cooking, use a clean fork or spoon.

Make sure work surfaces are clean and dry. This includes tables, worktops and chopping boards.

HOLi

The Spring festival of Holi falls when there is a full moon in late February or early March, during the Hindu month of Phalguna. This joyous festival is celebrated throughout India and everybody joins in.

The festival also celebrates the triumph of good over evil. People light huge bonfires to remember the time when the God, Vishnu, came down to earth as a man-lion. He saved his follower, Prahlad, from death in a bonfire and killed the evil tyrant who was tormenting him. In many villages, women carry their children round a bonfire asking Vishnu to protect them from evil in the months to come. Farmers may throw seeds on the bonfire and ask god to bless the crops that will be planted soon.

Holi is not a time to wear your best clothes. Everybody celebrates by throwing powdered dye and coloured water at each other. This sticks to clothes and hair. It takes a great many baths and hair-washes to get rid of it. Clothes are best thrown away after Holi! Paint is thrown as the festival remembers the time that the God, Krishna, playfully threw paint over the milkmaids and they threw paint over Krishna and his friends.

In India, it is hard to avoid the dye throwing in the street during Holi.

Revellers with coloured dye and water visit many houses. One way to avoid opening the door to a faceful of paint is to have plenty of snacks and hot drinks ready to feed the hungry revellers. The following pages show you how to make the sorts of foods that are often eaten in India during the Holi celebrations.

Making sweets for Holi in Jaipur, India. The most popular cooking method in India is frying in a deep pan called a *karhai*. The word 'curry' comes from *karhai*.

Samosas

Samosas are triangle-shaped parcels of food. Hindus fill them with vegetables; other people may use meat as well. They are a popular snack in many parts of the world and can be eaten hot or cold. Usually they are deep-fried, but this recipe cooks them in an oven, which is much safer.

Preparation time: 1 hour

Cooking time: 20–30 minutes

Oven temperature: 190 °C/ Gas Mark 5

Makes: 20 samosas

Ingredients

200 g potatoes

30 g carrots

2 tbsp ghee or oil

2 pinches ground turmeric

1/2 tsp chilli powder (optional)

1 tsp salt

2 tsp garam masala

100 g frozen peas, thawed

20 sheets of filo pastry, about 30 x 15 cm

Small bowl of oil for brushing filo pastry

Equipment

Saucepan

Chopping knife

Chopping board

Mixing bowl

Pastry brush

Baking tray

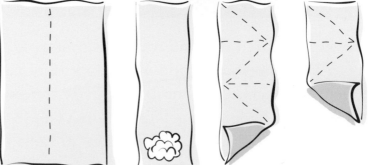

1 Peel the potatoes and carrots. Ask an adult to boil them for 5 minutes, so that they are part-cooked. Drain and let them cool down. Cut them into small pieces.

2 Put the vegetables into a bowl. Add the ghee or oil, turmeric, chilli powder (if using), salt, garam masala and peas. Stir well to mix.

3 Take a sheet of filo pastry and brush half of the strip with oil. Fold it in half lengthways and brush one corner with the oil.

4 Put 2 teaspoons of the vegetable mixture on the oiled end of the pastry and fold the pastry over diagonally, to make a triangle.

5 Fold the triangle over and over until all the pastry is used up. (See diagram, left.)

6 Place the samosas on an oiled baking tray and brush the tops with plenty of oil. Ask an adult to bake them for 20–30 minutes in the oven.

Onion Bhajis

Ingredients

3 large onions

7 tbsp vegetable oil

1 tsp mustard seeds

1/2 tsp ground turmeric

150 g gram (chick pea) flour

1/2 tsp salt

1/2 tsp chilli powder (optional)

Equipment

Chopping knife

Wooden spoon

Frying pan

Spatula

These fried onion cakes (bhajis, pronounced 'bar-jees') are eaten as a snack. People take them to eat on journeys or prepare them for unexpected guests. A plentiful supply of bhajis is a must at Holi. Normally, bhajis are deep-fried but these are shallow-fried for safety reasons.

1 Ask an adult to help you slice the onions.

2 Fry the mustard seeds and turmeric in 4 tablespoons of the oil until the seeds begin to pop.

3 Turn down the heat. Add the sliced onions and fry gently for another 10 minutes, until the onions are soft.

4 Add 1 tablespoon of the gram flour and stir. Do this again until all the gram flour has been used up.

5 Add the salt and chilli powder, (or some pepper if you don't use the chilli powder).

6 Take the mixture off the cooker to cool down. When it is cool, divide it into 4 pieces and mould each piece into a ball. Flatten the balls.

7 Ask an adult to heat the remaining oil and fry the bhajis, so that they get brown all over. Use a spatula to make sure they don't fall apart.

Garam Doodh

Cooking time: 10 minutes

Makes: 2 mugs

Ingredients

600 ml milk

2 tbsp honey

Pinch of grated nutmeg

Equipment

Milk pan

Spoon

This hot milk drink warms revellers on a cold Holi night. Festivals, such as Holi, that celebrate stories about Krishna, always involve food and drinks made from dairy products. Milk, butter and yoghurt were Krishna's favourite food and drink.

1 Put the milk in the pan and ask an adult to bring it to the boil.

2 Let the milk simmer for 5 minutes, without boiling over.

3 Take the milk off the heat and stir in the honey and nutmeg.

4 Pour carefully into mugs.

OTHER HOLI CELEBRATIONS

The spirit of Holi celebrations take over India, with many people joining in. Outside India this does not happen. In other countries, the Hindu communities do not have widespread Holi revels, as not everybody is Hindu and would welcome paint being thrown at them in the street!

The best Holi celebrations in the Western world are at ISKCON (Krishna Consciousness) centres. The statues of Krishna in the temple are dressed in festival clothes. Before the festival begins, members of the community spend hours in the kitchen preparing Krishna's favourite foods, which they offer to the statues in the temple and to people coming to join in the festivities. There is worship in the temple and revellers throw paint outside. In the evening there are plays about Krishna, his life among the milkmaids and cowherds, and the times he saved the world from evil.

During Holi celebrations in the UK, people cook coconuts in the traditional bonfire.

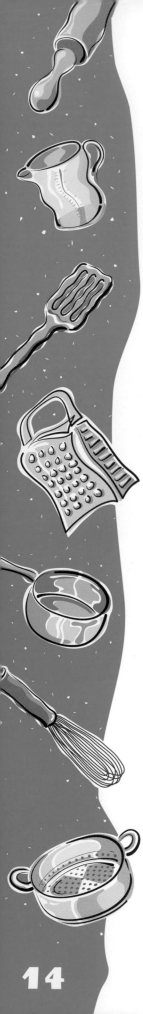

Divali

Divali means 'row of lights' and Divali is the Hindu festival of light. It falls in the Hindu month of Kartika which can occur either in October or November, depending on the cycle of the moon. Divali is celebrated all over India, and by Hindus in many other countries. Different stories and gods are remembered in different areas.

At Divali, Hindus draw colourful *rangoli* patterns using dyed rice flour.

Some people celebrate the time when Prince Rama was crowned king of Ayodhya after killing the evil tyrant, Ravana. When Rama returned to his kingdom, the roads were dark and people lit lamps at all the houses to guide him on his way.

Most people associate Divali with the Goddess of Fortune, Lakshmi. Everyone wants Lakshmi to visit his or her home at Divali to bring good fortune for the year to come. No effort is spared to entice her into the home. Houses are spring cleaned from top to bottom. Clay lanterns called *diwas* are lit at every door and window. Houses, shops and temples are covered in fairy lights.

Food plays an important part in the Divali festivities and sweets are prepared to exchange as gifts. Snacks are made to feed visitors calling with Divali cards and gifts. It is a time when families get together to feast and attend grand firework displays. These family feasts go on long into the night after the fireworks have finished.

A Hindu sweet shop sells hundreds of boxes of sweets each day before Divali.

15

Mattar Paneer

Preparation time: 10 minutes

Cooking time: 30 minutes

Serves: 6–8

Ingredients

275 g paneer

6 tbsp vegetable oil

2 onions

225 ml water

1/2 tsp salt

450 g peas

1 tsp sugar

2 tsp ground turmeric

1/2 tsp chilli powder

2 tsp dried ginger

1 tbsp fresh chopped coriander

Equipment

Karhai or frying pan

Wooden spoon

Chopping knife

Chopping board

Paper kitchen towel

Measuring jug

No festival vegetarian meal is complete without this dish of spiced vegetables and Indian cheese. Some people make a fresh batch of paneer every day to use in dishes such as this one, and in desserts. Paneer can be bought in Indian shops and some supermarkets. If you can't find it, you could use Italian mozzarella.

1 Cut the paneer into small cubes. Ask an adult to fry it in the oil until brown. Stir the cheese pieces so they get brown all over and don't stick to the pan.

2 When the cheese is brown take it out of the frying pan. Put it on a piece of kitchen towel to drain. Leave the rest of the oil in the pan.

3 Chop the onions finely. Ask an adult to put them in the pan and fry for 3–4 minutes, stirring all the time.

4 Add the water and salt and bring the mixture to the boil.

5 Add the peas and sugar and cover. Turn the heat down to a simmer. Cook the mixture for 10 minutes.

6 Add the paneer, turmeric, chilli and ginger and simmer for another 10 minutes, uncovered.

7 Put the mattar paneer in a serving dish and sprinkle the coriander over the top.

Pulao Rice with Peas and Nuts

Preparation time: 10 minutes

Cooking time: 30 minutes

Serves: 6–8

Ingredients

150 g basmati rice

4 tbsp ghee or oil

1 tsp cumin seeds

1 medium onion, sliced

4 cloves

1 tsp ground cinnamon

1 tsp garam masala

$1/2$ tsp salt

125 g frozen peas

25 g cashew nuts

25 g raisins

250 ml water

Equipment

Large bowl

Sieve

Large saucepan with a heavy bottom

Wooden spoon

Festive meals usually include pulao rice. The word 'pulao' (pronounced 'poolow') describes the method of cooking rice with vegetables and spices. The best rice to use for this dish is basmati rice. It stays light and fluffy, provided it is washed before cooking to get rid of extra starch that would make it sticky. Pulao rice goes well with the Mattar Paneer.

1 Put the rice in a bowl and carefully rinse in water. The water will go cloudy. Change the water a few times. When the water is clear, leave the rice to drain in a sieve.

2 Ask an adult to heat the ghee or oil in the saucepan with the cumin seeds.

3 After 3 minutes add the onion, cloves and cinnamon. Fry gently until the onion is brown.

4 Add the rice and fry for 2 minutes to get rid of the remaining water in the rice.

5 Stir in the garam masala, salt, peas, nuts and raisins.

6 Pour in the water and bring to the boil. Turn down to a simmer, stir, and cover the saucepan. Cook for 15 minutes. Take the pan off the heat and leave for 5 minutes, covered, before serving. This makes the rice nice and fluffy.

Coconut Barfi

Barfi (pronounced 'barfee') is a popular Indian sweet, which is always made for festivals. It's usually made by boiling sugar and milk together. This recipe is much easier to make, and is just as nice.

Preparation time: 20 minutes

Makes: 20 pieces

Ingredients

120 g honey

120 g peanut butter

80 g dates, finely chopped

85 g milk powder

130 g desiccated coconut

70 ml rose water

Equipment

Large mixing bowl

Small mixing bowl

Greaseproof paper

Cutting knife

Sweet tin

1 Mix the honey, peanut butter, dates and milk powder in a bowl using your hands. Make the sticky mixture into a non-sticky dough by kneading it. (Or ask an adult to mix the ingredients in a food processor.)

2 Roll the dough into a log about 50 cm long. Now wash your sticky hands and dry them well.

3 In the small mixing bowl, mix the coconut and the rose water.

4 Spread out the coconut and rose-water mixture on the greaseproof paper.

5 Cut the log in half and roll each half in the coconut so that it covers the log.

6 Cut each log into 10 pieces and store in the sweet tin. It will keep for about a week in the fridge. It tastes best if you take it out of the fridge about an hour before eating it.

OTHER DIVALI CELEBRATIONS

Hindus living outside India celebrate Divali with a flourish as it brings people together. The houses, shops and temples in Hindu areas are lit using clay lamps and fairy lights. Hindu temples become the focus for the celebrations and people travel great distances to celebrate Divali at the temple, and to meet up with family and friends who live a long way away.

Huge meals are prepared at Hindu temples for the large number of worshippers at Divali.

One of the best Divali celebrations is on the Caribbean island of Trinidad. Everybody on the island, even people who are not Hindu, such as Muslims and Christians, join in the celebrations. Divali becomes a carnival. The streets and buildings are lit, there are carnival processions and steel bands play on into the night. Stalls along the carnival route sell Caribbean food – curried goat and jerk chicken – as well as traditional Hindu snacks and curries.

GANESH CHATURTHI

This festival celebrates the birth of the elephant-headed god, Ganesh. It is said that Ganesh can remove any obstacles one might face. The festival is celebrated in late August or early September, which is during the Hindu month of Bhadra. Ganesh is a popular god and this festival is celebrated throughout India. It can last as long as seven to ten days.

A Ganesh festival procession in Hyderabad, India.

This painting of Ganesh shows him holding a bowl of his favourite sweets, ladoos.

During the festival, worshippers make a giant statue of Ganesh. The statue is paraded around a town and taken to a place where everyone can see it. Worshippers bring offerings of Ganesh's favourite foods. At the end of the festival, the statue is sunk in the sea, a lake or a river.

Everybody knows the story of Ganesh's favourite foods. Ganesh always travels in a chariot driven by a mouse. One night, Ganesh's mouse was frightened by a snake and the god fell out of his chariot. When he fell, his stomach burst open and the last food he had eaten – sweet rice pudding and ladoos (round sweet balls) – fell out. The moon laughed at Ganesh. This made the god angry. He tied up the hole in his stomach with the snake and cursed the moon. This story explains why the moon does not stay full all the time, but waxes and wanes.

During the festival, worshippers avoid looking at the moon for fear of offending Ganesh.

Kheer

Cooking time: 20 minutes

Oven temperature: 140 °C/
Gas Mark 1

Serves: 6

Ingredients

450 g tin ready-made rice
pudding, OR

   75 g round pudding rice

   1.2 litres milk

   2 tbsp sugar

250 ml milk

25 g sultanas

1 tbsp chopped almonds

1 tbsp ground pistachios

1/2 tsp ground cardamom

15 g sugar

1 tsp rosewater

Extra pistachios for decoration

Equipment

Oven dish

Saucepan

Spoon

Serving dish

Try this sweet rice pudding, even if you don't like puddings.
The spices make it taste wonderful! No wonder Ganesh,
who had a sweet tooth, found it irresistible.

1 If you cannot buy tinned rice pudding, make it in the oven: put the rice, 600 ml milk and 2 tbsp sugar into a heatproof dish. Put in the oven for 3 hours. After 1 hour, ask an adult to stir the pudding and add 300 ml more milk. Do the same after 2 hours.

2 Put the 250 ml milk in the saucepan. Carefully add the rice pudding from the tin, or the oven dish. Ask an adult to bring it to the boil.

3 Add the sultanas, almonds, pistachios, cardamom and sugar. Bring back to the boil.

Note: If you can't buy pistachios already ground, wrap a tablespoon of the
nuts in greaseproof paper and crush them using a rolling pin. They don't
have to be finely ground.

4 Reduce the heat and simmer the mixture for about 6 minutes, stirring so it does not stick.

5 Remove from the heat and stir in the rose water.

6 Put the mixture into a serving dish. Decorate the rice pudding by putting ground or chopped pistachio nuts on top. Eat it hot or cold.

Ladoos

Ladoos are sweet balls made from sugar, butter and flour. They are a popular sweet and a tin of these does not last long. Ganesh had eaten quite a number of ladoos when he fell out of his chariot.

Cooking time: 1 hour

Makes: 12–15 balls

Ingredients

250 g butter

285 g gram (chick pea) flour

1 1/2 tbsp grated/desiccated coconut

1 1/2 tbsp chopped walnuts or hazelnuts

1/2 tsp ground cardamom or cinnamon

180 g icing sugar

Equipment

Frying pan

Wooden spoon

Fork

1 Put the butter into the frying pan and ask an adult to melt it over a low heat.

2 Add the flour and stir with a wooden spoon over a gentle heat for 15 minutes to toast the flour. It is toasted when it has a nutty smell.

3 Stir in the coconut, the nuts and the cardamom/cinnamon. Fry for another 2 minutes and stir to mix in all the ingredients.

4 Take the pan off the heat. Add the icing sugar and mix well with a fork so there are no lumps. Leave to cool.

5 When the mixture is cool, moisten your hands and roll the mixture into 12 or 15 balls about 4 cm in diameter.

Scented Almond Drink

Ganesh Chaturthi occurs during the hot Indian summer and cool drinks are welcome both as offerings for Ganesh and for worshippers. Milk, or milk-like drinks, are thought to have spiritual qualities. This is why they are popular at festivals.

Preparation time: 1 hour

Cooking time: 20 minutes

Makes: 6 large drinks

Ingredients

100 g blanched almonds

1/2 tsp cardamom seeds

4 whole peppercorns

480 ml boiling water

4 tbsp honey

480 ml white grape juice

1/2 tbsp rose water

480 ml still or sparkling mineral water

Equipment

Mixing bowl

Measuring jug

Electric blender

Sieve

Cheesecloth

Jug

4 Put the sieve over a jug or bowl. Place the cheesecloth over the sieve and pour the mixture through the cheesecloth. The nut mixture will remain in the cheesecloth: you don't need this any more.

1 Put the almonds, cardamom seeds and peppercorns into a bowl. Add 300 ml of boiling water and leave to soak for an hour.

2 After an hour put the mixture into a blender and, with an adult's help blend it into a fine paste.

3 Add the honey and another 180 ml of boiled water and blend again.

5 Pour the nut milk into a jug. Add the grape juice, mineral water and rose water, and stir.

6 Put the jug into the fridge to chill before serving.

OTHER GANESH CHATURTHI CELEBRATIONS

Like so many Indian festivals outside India, Ganesh Chaturthi is a simple affair. Hindus visit their nearest temple to pay their respects to the statue of Ganesh. Hindu temples can be quite modest in countries other than India. Many are ordinary houses where one room is made into a temple. In areas where there is a large Hindu population, there might be a larger temple.

In India, temples are usually dedicated to one god. In other countries, the different gods may share a temple. For some Hindus who live a long way from their nearest temple the festival will be celebrated in the home. Most Hindu homes have a statue or picture of Ganesh as well as of other gods.

Making elephant masks for festival celebrations.

The gods are part of the family. They will be offered food before the family eat a meal and prayers will be said. Before making a journey, family members will always ask Ganesh's blessing. During the festival, family members will offer the statue or picture of Ganesh the ladoos, rice pudding, coconut and a drink as well as gifts of flowers.

FURTHER INFORMATION

The three festivals covered in this book are just a few of the many Hindu festivals celebrated in India, often at different times of the year. Other festivals include Maha Shiva Ratri (in honour of Shiva), Sarasvati Puja (first day of Spring), Rama Naumi (Rama's birthday), Ratha Yatra (in honour of Vishnu), Janmashtami (the birth of Krishna), and Navaratri (celebrating Durga). There are also many local festivals which are specific to a particular area.

> When using the recipes contained in this book, children should be supervised by one or more adults at all times. This especially applies when cutting with knives, cooking on a cooker hob and using the oven.

EQUIPMENT

The recipes are written on the understanding that adults have access to weighing and measuring equipment such as scales and measuring jugs. For clarity, these have not been shown in photos.

The traditional pan for frying Indian food is a *karhai* which looks like a Chinese wok with a thick bottom. Using a wok or a *karhai* with children is not always a good idea as they are easy to tip over during cooking. A thick bottomed frying pan will be safer and easier to use.

Indian food is served on *thali* dishes. These are small pots on a large tray. Many shops sell these, or it is easy to improvise, using pudding bowls on a large tray.

Hindus eat meals with their right hand instead of cutlery. The left hand is used for personal hygiene, including going to the toilet. It's important to wash before eating.

COOKING METHODS

The traditional Hindu method of cooking snacks such as samosas and onion bhajis is to deep-fry them in the *karhai*. For safety reasons, in this book they have been shallow-fried or cooked in the oven. Sweets such as barfi are normally boiled using a mixture of hot sugar, water and milk powder. Again, for safety reasons, a cold method of making barfi has been used in place of a traditional recipe.

Samosas: initially, the way of wrapping the triangles may seem rather complicated, but it is easily mastered, with practice. See the diagram on page 8.

Chilli powder is optional in recipes as some children don't like hot food. If you do use chilli, stress the safety aspect of working with it. Children must not touch the chilli and then put their hands to their eyes. If this happens, rinse out the eye liberally with water.

INGREDIENTS

NB: Nuts, contained in some recipes in this book, may provoke a severe allergic reaction in some people.

Rice: Always try to use basmati rice in Hindu cooking as it stays separated after cooking and does not become heavy or stodgy like other kinds of rice.

Ghee: Use this for cooking if you can. Ghee is clarified butter made from cows' milk. All the milk solids have been removed so that ghee can be heated to a high temperature without any risk of burning. It also does not need to be kept in a fridge. However, if you can't find it, use sunflower oil instead.

Paneer: (can also be spelt panier) This is Indian curd cheese. It is made by curdling milk, separating the white curds and pressing them into a cheese. It is sometimes sold already cut into pieces, and sometimes as a whole piece. If you can't find this use mozzarella or Greek *hallumi* cheese instead. If you use paneer be careful as it goes off very quickly. It also sticks very easily to the cooking pan: take care to stir it constantly while frying.

Gram flour: This is made from ground chick peas and can be bought in Indian shops. It is pale yellow and has a sweet, nutty flavour. It is best to use this for ladoos if at all possible, but if you cannot buy it, an alternative may be US-style cornmeal.

Garam masala: A ready-made mixture of spices (cardamon, cinnamon, cloves, cumin, coriander and black peppercorns).

TOPIC WEB

Science
Food and nutrition
Changing materials through heat
Separating/mixing of materials

English
Write a menu for a Hindu meal
Traditional stories of Hindu gods
Hindu/Indian poetry

Geography
India: location/features/farming/
seasons/weather/culture
Cycles of the moon

Maths
Using and understanding
data/measures/fractions
Using measuring instruments

History
Indian migration worldwide
History of India

Design and Technology
Design a set of balancing scales
Make a storage box for sweets
Design a poster for Hindu food

RE
Hindu beliefs and worship
Hindu lunar calendar
Numerous Hindu festivals

Modern Foreign Languages
Variety of Indian languages
Indian words adopted into other
languages

GLOSSARY

Cowherds People who look after a small number of cows.

Dairy Describes foods made from animals' milk, such as cheese, yoghurt and butter.

Emigrate When people leave their own country and go to live in another country.

Ganesh The elephant-headed god who removes obstacles from the path of religious life.

Karhai A Hindu frying pan. It looks like a Chinese wok.

Krishna An incarnation of the God Vishnu. Krishna was brought up in a village with cowherds and milkmaids. He loves cows, and food made from dairy products such as milk, butter and yoghurt.

Paneer Indian curd cheese.

Prashad Sacred food that is offered to the gods.

Rama One of the incarnations of Vishnu, who appeared as an Indian prince.

Rangoli **patterns** Brightly coloured patterns made from rice flour that are used to decorate pathways at Divali. The patterns are usually of sacred Hindu symbols and flowers.

Reincarnation People who die being reborn as another human, animal, bird, fish or insect.

Spices Vegetable extracts used to flavour food, such as chilli, turmeric and ginger.

Statue A figure of a god, person or animal. Statues can be made out of materials such as stone, metal, wood or clay and painted with colours.

Temple A building where a god or gods are worshipped.

Thali A selection of small bowls placed on a large tray. Hindus often eat their food from a *thali*.

Tyrant A cruel ruler.

Vegetarian Somebody who does not eat meat or fish.

Vishnu One of the three most important Hindu gods. He is the protector of the world and is often considered God Himself.

INDEX

Page numbers in **bold** refer to photographs

RESOURCES

Books

Celebrate Hindu Festivals by Dilip Kadodwala and Paul Gateshill (Heinemann, 1995)
Festivals: Divali by Kerena Marchant (Hodder Wayland, 1999)
Hinduism by Katherine Prior and Dilip Kadodwala (Franklin Watts, 1995)
Holi by Dilip Kadodwala (Evans Brothers, 1997)
Madhur Jaffrey's Illustrated Indian Cookery by Madhur Jaffrey (BBC, 1996)
Quick and Easy Indian Vegetarian by Veena Chopra (Foulsham, 1995)

Web sites

http://www.hindunet.org
The Hindu Universe: features a Hindu calendar, a glossary of terms and information on Hindu arts, customs and worship.
http://india.indiagov.org/culture/religion/hinduism.htm
Hinduism: An Eclectic Religious Tradition. Maintained by the Indian government; gives information on Hindu beliefs and festivals.
http://www.iskcon.org.uk/ies/: See ISKCON, right.

Useful addresses

ISKCON Educational Services
Bhaktivedanta Manor
Hilfield Lane, Aldenham, Watford, Herts WD2 8EZ
Tel: 01923 859578
email: ies@com.bbt.se
Runs programmes for schools; largest supplier of educational resources on Hinduism in Britain, with mail-order service.

The Commonwealth Institute Resource Centre
Kensington High Street, London W8 6NQ
Tel: 020 7603 4535
http://www.commonwealth.org.uk

The Institute of Indian Art and Culture
The Bhavan Centre
4a Castletown Road, London W14 9HQ
Tel: 020 7381 3045

The Hindu Cultural Society
321 Colney Hatch Lane, London N11
Tel: 020 8361 4484